EDUCATORS ON THE FRONTLINES

IMPLICIT BIAS UNDER
Structural combative
Long Hours Parents PAID
 Lack of
Racism Work-Life Imbalance
TOO MANY Resources Policies
ROLES! Over-Crowded
 MicroAggressions
UNAPPRECIATED Classrooms
Stress

A Self-Care Guide for Teachers & Administrators

Maati Wafford, MSW
Jeff Menzise, Ph.D.

Educators on the Frontlines: A self-care guide for teachers and administrators.

Copyright ©2019 by Jeff Menzise. All rights reserved. Printed in the United States of America. No part of this book may be used or reproduced in any manner without written permission from the author except in the case of brief quotations embodied in critical articles and reviews. For information address Mind on the Matter Publishing, Post Office Box 755, College Park, Maryland 20741.

10 9 8 7 6 5 4 3 2 1

Cover Design by Jeffery Menzise, Ph.D. for Mind on the Matter Publishing

Library of Congress Cataloging-in-Publication Data
Menzise, Jeffery,
    Educators on the Frontlines: A self-care guide for teachers and administrators. / by Maati Wafford, MSW and Jeff Menzise, Ph.D.
includes Introduction, Main Text, Cover and Internal Artwork, & Design

ISBN 978-0-578-61706-0

Published in 2019 by
Radiant Mind Solutions, an imprint of
Mind on the Matter Publishing,
PO BOX 755, College Park, MD 20741
Website: www.radiantmindsolutions.com
Email: radiantmindsolutions@gmail.com
Office Phone: 202-813-9079

Acknowledgments

We would first like to acknowledge the long line of ancestral and living educators who have dedicated their lives to revolutionizing education by fearlessly demanding justice from themselves and the larger society. These educators paved the way for us to be able to have the difficult conversations of today. Through their sacrifice, we are here today, standing tall and seeking to improve education, educators, and the educated by any means necessary. We pray that this guide is received with an open mind and an open heart, and that our intentions are understood to reflect our desire for the best there is to offer for the future generations of humankind.

Next, we send a large thank you to the independent educational institutions who thrive while maintaining their integrity, unapologetically and constantly going through intentional self-refinement seeking to provide premium services to the children in their care. We also acknowledge and thank our families who continue to support our endeavors by seeking our expertise, and by sharing their valuable insights regarding education.

Dedication

This guide is dedicated to all front line educators. Whether teachers, administrators, support staff, or parents, we value your contribution and recognize your importance. We have written this guide with you in mind. We hope that you find inspiration, motivation, and a renewed sense of dedication and devotion to your calling as an educator. We hope that within these pages, you find practical insight and applicable tools that you can relate to, and that enhance your well-being both in your everyday personal life, as well as in your professional roles. Have the courage to grow and change...and dare to put yourself first.

Table of Contents

Introduction..pg. 7

Tip	Page No.
#1 Meditation	11
#2 Physical Well-Being	17
#3 Establish Boundaries	23
#4 Be Still	29
#5 Self-Awareness	35
#6 Be Creative	41
#7 Be Productive	47
#8 Unite With Like-Minds	53
#9 Maintain Hobbies	59
#10 Pursue Professional Development	65

Positive Growth Affirmations..............pg. 71

About The Authors...................................pg. 72

> Children Learn More From What You Are Than What You Teach.
> – W.E.B. DuBois

As a child, I was very excited about the roles teachers played. I am not quite sure where the inspiration came from; I don't recall any one teacher who I admired, nor do I remember imagining to be anyone other than the grown-up, professional, teacher-version of myself. I would go all out in my role play. At the beginning of the scene, I ALWAYS had to call my class to attention, because of course, we know how rowdy those Cabbage Patch Kids and Barbie Dolls can be. After the cadre of well-mannered dolls were sitting faced-forward and attentive at their "desks," I would proceed with announcing the day's lesson. "Today, class, we are going to learn about numbers and how to add them together..."

This was perhaps my favorite game to play at nine-years-old. My little self was mesmerized by playing the role of teacher. I felt empowered to know something and to be able to teach my doll-students. Even at that young age, I realized that I was doing more than shaping their intellect, I was also helping to create new people. I loved that teaching involved bound and determined attention to details. I had to ensure that I had all the required tools such as: special ordered chalk holders, a big calendar with fancy pens, and perhaps most importantly, high-heeled shoes that would make lots of noise announcing my arrival as I walked down the hallway. I would also need a shiny ceramic apple with my last name displayed prominently on my desk, with a small bottle of Jergens lotion tucked away in the middle drawer to keep my hands moisturized between lessons. Without a doubt, I had to have a lot of paper, a stapler, a hole puncher, and some white out. If I was lucky, I could catch a ride with my grandma on her Saturday trip to the bank, which doubled as my supply center. Inside, not only did they give you a lollipop, but there was an oasis of rectangular slips of paper and small envelopes that were mine for the taking. I also loved getting a hold of those cool carbon paper pads that my grandfather used to play "the numbers." These were extra cool because I was able to sometimes see the math he had performed in the previous week. This gave me an opportunity to grade his work. I sit back with appreciation that even as a child, my eyes noticed so many details about what teachers did and what they needed to be successful: paper, pens, pumps, and maybe a projector. But was that all there was to it? Nope.

After growing older, obtaining advanced degrees, and spending many years observing and engaging in the art, science, and craft of teaching and school leadership, I came to that "shocking" realization that much more is required. My perspective definitely shifted as I became more and more aware of the various methods for teaching; and I definitely changed my mind about those pumps...I'll take a pair of flats any day! Although I still spy a nice pair or two on a colleague and smile when I hear that clicking sound they make as she walks the halls.

This book is written in honor of those faithful, highly-skilled educators and school administrators, who have a tremendous impact on the health of society and ultimately influence human evolution. It takes courage to successfully take on such an extensive role and heavy responsibility. The fact that we do it implies that we are at least willing to uphold high standards, that we have the potential for outstanding character strength, and that we also possess physical and mental health and vitality. How else could a person live up to the awesome task of teaching and leading schools, developing the minds of generations to come?

The purpose of this book is to inspire, as we aspire to validate the importance of the educator, by bringing much needed awareness to how teachers and administrators can persevere and find ongoing cycles of fulfillment in a career that is often highly criticized, simultaneously overlooked, and dare I say undervalued. Our society is plagued with poverty, racism, and a troubled education system that often weighs heavy on the hearts and minds of teachers and school administrators alike. Subsequently meditation and healthy living, while increasing your overall awareness of these societal ills, can equip you with the inner balance and stability needed to rise above the issues. Being emotionally connected with students and their families can be taxing, so we thought it important to develop this guide to assist our fellow educators to be careful on the front lines.

Being unaware of the complex nature of inequity, especially as it manifests within our schools, can make it challenging for educators to navigate situations that may arise within their domain of influence. By developing a healthy understanding of the systematic nature of racism/white supremacy, microaggressions, and implicit biases, you will elevate your sense of discernment, which then serves to protect you from the pitfalls of self-blame, frustration, and confusion. Although this guide is not designed for a deep dive into these issues, we will highlight numerous actions that can be implemented to buffer their deleterious effects.

Needless to say, it is imperative for educators to have outlets for healthy expression and rejuvenation. Self-care is the major and on-going theme of this book. It is the key to a long lasting, healthy career. We encourage educators to do some soul searching, and to create spaces while allowing time for self-reflection. Once you have successfully addressed your "stuff," you are then more capable of being fully present in our classrooms and schools. Sometimes this experience comes through some sort of yoga practice, or perhaps via meditative, exercising, or even reading. For others it is found in their religious ceremonies, deep breathing, prayer, affirmations, journaling, or a combination of any of these. Regardless of how it comes, the goal is to carve out space and time for re-centering; for your body to release stress and tension, and for you to calm yourself, letting go of the ruminating thoughts, and thereby entering into deeper states of relaxation.

The flow of the book is designed to engage you both verbally as well as symbolically. We have aesthetically developed a pattern that will keep your brain engaged while also prompting your mind into deeper levels of thinking about common topics. You will notice that each "self-care" section includes a "visual cue" page that offers a symbolic image and written reminders. This page functions as a great "at-a-glance" snapshot tool, for you to gain a holistic understanding of that particular tip.

The "sticky notes" serve as promptings, pointing to other self-care tips that are interrelated and provide opportunities for deeper exploration. For example, when we look at the visual cue in the section on meditation (see image above), we are being encouraged to internalize and reflect on how Being Still, Creativity, Physical Well-Being, and Self Awareness all connect with the overall processes and purpose of our meditation practice. When one commits to meditation, they are also directly and indirectly engaging their physical well-being. Self Awareness and meditation are also closely related; in fact, many use meditation for this reason. Creativity serves the visualization aspect of meditation, where symbolic representations are common. And finally, stilling the mind and body are normal by-products of meditation.

Allow us to lead you along an organic path towards inner peace and productivity. We offer you this "go-to resource" for when you are in need of a quick anchor to get rooted, retooled, and reinvigorated as you continue to show up, on purpose, to serve and direct the leaders of tomorrow. - Maati

Self-Care Tip #1

MEDITATION

Thanks to the recent campaigns promoting meditation, almost everybody and their momma has at least heard of it. This ancient art is now so popular that meditation smart phone apps have their own commercials; while academic research brought it into the ivory towers, and into the board rooms of corporate America. This added "scientific" credibility has brought meditation out of the dreaded category of being a pseudoscience, right onto the prestigious list of "best practices." In schools across the United States, we are seeing an increased use of meditation both as a means for preventing disciplinary problems, and for intervening once problems have been identified. Professional athletes and franchises are also discussing how they benefit from various forms of meditation. NBA superstar Steph Curry, who served as the face for Kaiser's promotion of meditation as a viable tool, is probably the best known example of this phenomenon.

What we find in this popularization of meditation is the simplification of an otherwise complex system, which typically requires an almost monk-like devotion in order to have any notable effects. By modernizing meditation, many "short-cuts" have been introduced alongside a non-religious approach to the practice. This is

> The Power Of Meditation Is Its Universal Appeal And The Fact That It Can Be Applied To Anything That Is Done With Intention.

important because it brings meditation out of the sometimes inaccessible realm of spirituality, and into the more comprehensible, practically-applicable and tangible world of our everyday modern lives. What we have is a form of meditation, distilled from volumes of philosophical lore, that is both easy to decipher and apply.

The power of meditation, in part, is its universal appeal and the fact that it can be applied to anything that is done with intention. This means that your entire life—personal, professional, emotional, psychological, intellectual, and even the anatomical and physiological—can benefit from a consistent meditation practice.

One of the main by-products of meditation is the "slowing down of time." This commonly reported experience is an indication that the practitioner is perceiving life in smaller segments, as opposed to the day passing by as a giant blur. Perceiving life in smaller increments usually coincides with the slowing down of thoughts, movement, and even the amount of time it takes to respond-react to stimulation. This "slowing down" will help you to understand the inner workings of experiences and interactions with people. Meditation becomes a most valuable tool for everyday use because, as teachers and administrators, we engage people everyday, all day. It allows us to slow down, truly listen, take the time to reflect and answer a question, respond to situations thoughtfully, and live our lives on purpose.

Imagine moving through your professional life enjoying the heightened ability to perceive your options and make the most appropriate decisions, while fully observing the interrelatedness of all variables. Not only will you be less likely to make mistakes, but the damage and fallout from those that do occur, is minimized and usually reparable. You will also experience an improvement in your efficiency and effectiveness. This translates into you being able to complete more work with less energy, accomplish goals at a greater rate, and spend less time confused, frustrated, and stagnated.

As you will see, meditation is a valuable tool that can be used to enhance and support several other tips shared throughout this guide. You will also notice how meditation itself is enhanced by the mastery and application of some of these same tips. For example, improving physical health requires discipline and a strong will. Discipline and the development of a strong will are enhanced by meditation. Likewise, meditation as a practice, benefits from a state of physical health and wellbeing. The intentional breathing, relaxation, and perspective shifting associated with meditation is known to improve blood pressure, psychological distress, and other ailments incurred as a result of living life.

Seek out the various methods of meditation and test out a few. Once you find the "brand" and method that works best for you, set your intentions on making the practice consistent. On the following pages, we provide you with some insights to consider as you go about becoming more familiar with meditation, and its application to your professional and personal life. These points are consistent and applicable to most meditative practices and can be taken as a whole, or separated into individual chunks, based on what best serves your intentions. As with any exercise, you should seek the guidance of your licensed health care practitioner before beginning.

1. Breathe on Purpose

Find a comfortable rate of breathing that allows you to increase your breathing capacity. For example, inhale for 3 seconds, hold the breath for 3 seconds, then exhale for 3 seconds. Slowly increase the length of your inhale, exhale, and hold, each by one second. This will greatly assist with relaxation, and improve your vitality.

2. Get Comfortable

Many beginners start off practicing in the comfort of their own beds or some specially designated space in their homes. Although meditation does not require a formal setting, it is sometimes easier to get started by identifying a place specifically set-aside for a daily practice. Once you advance, you will begin to recognize that meditation, in some form or another, can be practiced almost anywhere.

3. Be Consistent

Establishing a daily practice is of extreme importance. In order to obtain maximum benefits from meditation, practitioners must make the meditative state habitual and a default state of mind. Like any other tool, gift, or talent, improving one's skill and competency is based upon training, consistent practice, and by constantly seeking to grow and improve. You can start small with a 5 minute per day practice; perhaps using the first few minutes of your daily morning routine.

4. Establish Affirming Words

Affirmations, also called Mantra, are designed to "protect the mind" from wayward and counterproductive thoughts while meditating. Having a consistent go-to phrase will also assist with focusing on the meditative goal by constantly reminding you of your expected outcome. At the end of this book, we have provided some powerful self-care affirmations. Try by repeating these during your meditation.

5. Set Clear and Manageable Goals

Although there are forms and methods of meditating that encourage practitioners to "drift" and allow their minds to roam wherever it may go, there are other forms designed to achieve specific outcomes; In the case of the latter, it is important for practitioners to be clear about those objectives, and resolute in their desire to achieve them. Clearly thought out and stated goals are much easier to focus on than a long drawn out stew of desires.

6. Relax

Relaxation is both a by-product and facilitator of meditation. Enter into your practice as relaxed as possible. Warm showers and baths, essential oils, and various teas may help. The regulated breathing exercises suggested above, in conjunction with the mantra to keep your mind focused should get you off to a great start.

Self-Care Tip #2

PHYSICAL WELL-BEING

Physical well-being is perhaps the most tangible of all the self-care tips presented in this guide. Without an intentional focus on our physical health, we can let it slip away like a hat in high winds. Unlike that hat, once the downward spiral of compromised health gets beyond a certain point, it can be impossible to restore or replace. Because our job, as educators, is often stressful and filled with the daily exchange of a plethora of energies from those in our care, it becomes imperative for us to be conscious of our own health, and vigilant in the protection of the same.

This particular tip goes beyond cold and flu prevention, and being sure to wash your hands thoroughly and regularly throughout the day. Instead, it involves those deeper aspects of our physical selves that are directly related to our psychological and emotional states. This interdependent perspective of the mind-body relationship is what brings the necessary holistic understanding into the forefront of our minds when contemplating how to improve and maintain ourselves in a state of optimal health.

The physical taxation experienced by educators is often ignored and overlooked by those working in a seemingly stress free environment. This can be just as, or even

> Without Our Physical Health, Our Mental Health And Well-being Are Bound To Suffer.

more dangerous than working in an environment with known toxicity. This is because an awareness of hazardous conditions usually increases the likelihood that people will avoid and/or prepare against those elements. Those who are not aware, are more likely to ignore the subtle signs that they are, in-fact, swimming in a septic ooze. The typical ingredients of this ooze include: microaggressions, incompetent and unethical leadership, a lack of defined roles, and tension between parents, teachers, and administrators. This environment is set up to produce a lack of receptivity, defensiveness, tension, and a perpetual stream of psychological and physiological stress. Knowing that one is in a toxic workplace, they are more likely to take on the defensive stance required to preserve what little is left of their health and vitality.

Unfortunately, many people (including educators) find unhealthy ways of coping with their daily stressors, which ultimately compound the negative effects of stress on physical health. For example, those who turn to the consumption of alcohol to relax, tend to become dependent on "having a drink" for relaxation. For this reason, it is important to incorporate a majority of stress relieving practices that not only produce no harm, but also provide beneficial effects on your physical well-being.

In our previous tip, we mentioned how the practice of meditation directly impacts overall stress levels, which in turn positively impacts blood pressure and many stress related ailments. We also mentioned how there is a bi-directional relationship between many of the tips conveyed throughout this guide. In the case of physical well-being and its impact on meditation, we find that a body that is relatively free from dis-ease, is more apt to maintaining the vitality necessary for a powerful meditation session. This is not to say that people who are suffering from acute and chronic illness do not experience deep meditations, because they absolutely do, all we are saying is that a healthy body facilitates a healthy mind, which in turn facilitates our ability to benefit from a consistent meditation practice.

The preservation and restoration of physical well-being is one of the main goals of this guide. Without our physical health, our mental health and well-being are bound to suffer. For this reason, we have developed holistic health tips for both the mind and body. Educators who find the time to implement the following, will surely find themselves in a better place in both their professional and personal lives.

- Self-Awareness
- Professional Development
- Meditation
- Unify With Like Minds

1. Learn More About Health and Healing

Use some of your spare reading and learning time to study health and well-being. This includes learning about vitamins & minerals, supplements, and the medical history of your own family. Think about incorporating health-related facts and information into the lessons you teach. Wellness can be infused into any lesson...math, science, literature, history, etc. Have fun with it, and get well while doing it.

2. Exercise Regularly and Often

Establishing a regular exercise routine, no matter how rigorous, will serve to improve your vitality, sense of self, and self-esteem. Do something to increase your strength and heart rate daily. This can be as simple as knocking out a few jumping jacks, burpees, or push-ups in the morning. Or a brisk walk around the block. Do something, and do it often.

3. Improve Your Diet

"Food As Medicine" is an age-old concept that is no longer as popular as it once was. Convenience and taste have taken priority over nutritional value and health benefits. Of the many health related variables that are beyond our control, it is to our advantage to firmly grasp those things that we can control; what we eat is one of those things. Being disciplined, selective, knowledgeable, and unapologetic about wanting to improve your physical health by controlling your diet is a courageous first step. Learning to prepare a variety of health-positive meals, and actually making them, can be fun and physically empowering to you and those you care about.

4. Look to Nature

Did you know that many pharmaceuticals are derived from naturally occurring substances? Yup! The headache and pain-relieving effects of aspirin come from the curative properties of the white willow tree. Numerous pharmaceutically-based treatments were, and are, actually discovered by scientists observing "indigenous" societies addressing their own illnesses. Why not take this same approach to your own health? Consider looking to nature, herbal remedies, holistic health, and nature-based practices for a new perspective on health and healing. This does not mean that you should ditch your regularly scheduled visits to your doctor; nor does it mean to avoid filling your prescriptions. This is a gentle nudge to become more knowledgeable and empowered when it comes to taking care of your physical health and well-being.

5. Seek the Advice of Healthcare Professionals

It is ALWAYS beneficial to have experts on your team. People who are knowledgeable about a particular subject are great resources for finding answers to questions, gaining an understanding of information, and to provide primary, secondary, and sometimes tertiary opinions on matters of health. Your licensed health care provider is a great partner to employ in your quest for optimal health.

6. Prioritize Personal Hygiene

Embedded within this suggestion is the elimination of negative and detrimental habits from your daily routine. This requires us to have an objective view of our choices, and the ability to walk away from any that we deem to be detrimental to our well-being. This includes people, activities, attitudes, and perspectives as well as our own behaviors.

Self-Care Tip #3

ESTABLISH BOUNDARIES

Having and respecting boundaries is a natural part of life. Nature is filled with examples of boundary-setting, and the benefit of respecting those that have been established. Think of how a river is defined by its banks. The river flows through the natural boarders set by the earth, while simultaneously shaping these boundaries, and therefore, its own course. This interplay between the boundary and the bound is also recognizable by the presence of eroded soil found floating in the water, as it is transported to new lands by way of the river. This analogy demonstrates how integrity is maintained, and power gained, by the limiting aspect of boundaries.

This limiting effect provides a predictable focus, a consolidation of power, and a sense of direction for those willing to submit to the inevitability of the existence of parameters in all that we do. The favorable effects of boundaries are observable in the difference between a flamethrower and a blow torch. The former provides an awesome display of fire that will bedazzle and entertain the curious eye. The latter is much smaller and a lot less grand in its display of focused flame, however, the power inherent in its fire cannot be denied.

> We All Learned To Color Within The Lines Way Back In Kindergarten.

The flame thrower will have a hard time cutting through steel; sure it would heat the metal quite nicely, but would hardly begin to cut through it. The blow torch, on the other hand, exhibits in the power of focused-heat, what the flamethrower beautifully displayed with its widely distributed flames. Manipulating the form of the fire, allows us to harness the power of the heat by limiting and concentrating its range of expression.

Our professional and personal lives similarly benefit and become more efficient and effective through the skillful application of boundaries and limitations. For example, as educators it is easy to become distracted by the multitude of non-teaching related requirements of a healthy and productive classroom. It is easy to get pulled into yet another committee, another task, another meeting, or another opportunity to volunteer, without thinking twice about the already impressive mound of duties and responsibilities related to your classroom and/or area of administration. The nature of an educator is to help people; this is why we are ripe for the picking when it comes to soliciting our help and accessing our already tapped resources.

Not only do we boundlessly give of our time, as demonstrated by our willingness to work a full school day, then bring home papers to grade (and arrive early the next day for preparation), but we are also willing to pay for needed materials and supplies out of our own pockets. Sure educators are often given a "tax break" for items bought for their classrooms and/or schools, but a tax break does not alleviate the burden in real-time. Add to this the stress associated with your perceived value and competency (merit) being directly tied into the performance of the students and school. As educators, we often find ourselves in a bind; caught between making consistent and constant sacrifices and the desire and thought to just let it go. The best way to address this burdensome cycle is to cut it off and reestablish boundaries in ways that are mutually beneficial and most importantly, non-injurious to educators and their families.

In this day and age being adept at forming healthy parameters around your home and work life is imperative. If we could only choose a few words to encapsulate the teaching profession "devotion" would certainly be at the top of this list. For those of us who are truly called to teach and lead schools, being steadfast and unwavering will often bring us accolades and acknowledgments. However, being known as the overachieving, always reliable, working on weekends, constantly on-call type of educator can and will put a strain on you as a professional, particularly when you have not created firm boundaries that allow for your own rejuvenation and renewal. Sadly, we usually see this in others before we recognize it playing out in our own lives.

While not always an easy thing to do for empathic and sympathetic educators, establishing boundaries ultimately benefits all parties involved in the long run. It helps to prevent teacher burnout, while exhibiting an attitude of self-respect, which then encourages others to respect you, your time, and your personal resources. The following suggestions are designed to take the guesswork out of boundary setting by providing clear and easy to apply tips when gearing up to lay down the law.

- Be Still
- Unify With Like Minds
- BOUNDARY
- Be Productive
- Professional Development

1. Know Your Value and Self-Worth

When you are doing a job that you absolutely love and have a role in which you want to excel, you may find the lines slowly being blurred. Sure there are many things that you are qualified, capable, and willing to do. However, in your quest to make a change, and demonstrate your expertise while serving your community, you are also at risk of losing sight of your organizational value. Having a healthy sense of what you are bringing to the table and how that value can and should be compensated equitably, gives you a holistic view of your professional value, which boosts your confidence and self-worth.

2. Know and Own your Job Description

Ask yourself, "what am I actually being paid to do?" And then, just do that! And if you find yourself consistently doing more, ask for a job title and the compensation that reflects what you actually do. This does not mean to be so rigid that you never assist or offer to serve above and beyond the call of duty. What we are saying here is to always be willing and capable of unapologetically sticking to the plan.

3. Know Where to Draw the Line

When you are crystal clear about your job and the role you signed up for, you are equipped to know each time you are asked to step outside of that to do more. With your growing mindfulness practice, you will know when this is happening and understand that you are always making a choice to do more. The reality is, we all tend do more. Knowing where and when to draw the line is a practice worth mastering.

4. Develop Positive Ways to Articulate Your Boundaries

This is the fun part. How can you honor your boundaries and still be eloquent and distinct with colleagues and administration? Calling on your improving self-awareness skills is key. If you find yourself tensing up, clenching your fists, or holding your breath, these are clear signs that you are not ready to articulate a boundary. Remember your meditation routines. Breathe through the tension and allow yourself time to center before replying to that email or answering that question. When feeling pressed, one of the best ways to respond is
"Let me get back to you."

5. Choose Acquaintances that are Supportive and Affirming

The company that you keep is absolutely important because these are the major sources of your social influence, and are also those by which you may be judged. To have an inner circle that is protective, supportive, and affirming is to have a bit of a buffer-zone between you and the outside world. These are the people who screen the access that others have to you. On the other hand, if this core group of acquaintances is sketchy, drama-filled, and stressful to you and your world, you should consider revising the circumference of that circle to only include those you trust to be considerate of your time, professionalism, and the reputation you desire for yourself.

Self-Care Tip #4

BE STILL

Of all the self-care tips presented within this guide, this is, perhaps, the most difficult to achieve. On the surface, stillness seems to be as simple as it gets. I mean, there's not much to sitting in one place for a period of time, not moving, right? Give it a try. Take the next 15 seconds and remain as still as possible. Notice how your intention to remain still interfered with your ability to do so. Did you begin to feel the "creepy crawlies"? The sensation that something was crawling on your arm? A random itch on your face? Did you have to adjust your posture at all? Now how about your mind? Were you able to keep that still as well? Did you even try?

It is perfectly okay if you have faced challenges similar to those mentioned above. In fact, it is to be expected for those of us who are new to intentional "stillness." The ability to achieve stillness, in both mind and body, is of great importance when it comes to physical, psychological, and emotional health. Not only does it provide the necessary relaxation of our bodies, but it also affords us the space to slow down our thinking to the point of no longer having a thought, or a sense of mental restlessness.

> Seeking Out Stillness, Incorporating Mindfulness Routines, & Paying Close Attention To Our Diets, All Contribute To Healthy Preparation Of The Mind, Spirit, And Body Temple.

As educators, rarely do we find that space to do absolutely nothing. Rarely do we experience the state of mind where there is absolutely nothing fighting for priority. On the contrary, we are often consumed with the concerns and priorities set by the beautiful souls (our students) to whom we have pledged our allegiance. When we aren't tending to them, we are usually preparing to tend to them. If we are not occupied by preparation, then we are usually tied up trying to squeeze in a bit of a personal life. None of this is still.

Feeling rushed, mentally exhausted, generally overwhelmed, having the sense that your days are running together, are all indicative of needing to slow down. I have often warned clients that it is "better to choose to slow down, before life forces you to." This forced down-shift comes in many forms, but usually manifest in physical ailments such as an injury (broken bone or strained tendon), or even in the form of some sort of illness (cold, flu, or something a little more serious). Regardless of the form, the outcome is usually the same…bed rest. I recently spoke with a client, that is also an educator, who exclaimed with a hint of pride how she "ENJOYED my two weeks off while healing from my shoulder surgery." Imagine that. Being in the painful stages of recovery was somehow enjoyable in comparison to the daily grind she experienced as an educator and administrator in a public school system.

It is fascinating to see how easily we can be distracted by the world around us. This is especially intriguing amongst the more "learned" of us; specifically those of us who serve others. It is my firm belief that when people have a desire to serve others, and subsequently develop the skills to be proficient at such, it is most beneficial to first apply the new knowledge, skills, and competencies to our own lives, before setting out to make our mark on the world. For those who do the opposite, meaning they eagerly rush to "save the world" before applying their newly developed skills on themselves, tend to suffer from what we like to call "being seduced by the external."

The external seduction is a powerful force that is both subtle in its approach and detrimental in its impact. Many of us are immediately drawn into helping others by way of giving advice and providing guidance and lessons, because this is often easier than doing the work on ourselves. It is also a natural function of the nurturing, "need-to-be-needed" aspect of those of us who "choose" helping professions. We must resist the urge to jump out there, and take some time with ourselves. It's like they say on the airplane, put your mask on first!!! This is best done by remaining internally still, and externally slow to action. Ever notice how in those "old school" Kung Fu flicks the elder Master is almost always calm when being tested by the younger aggressor? Or how in a bank robbery scene, the hero is always the one shown remaining calm throughout the ordeal? This is the essence of keeping still, it gives you the advantage of a lucid mind, and calmness of emotions and actions.

We'd like to offer one last example of the power of stillness before moving on. In the movie "Return to the 36 Chambers" the young monk wants to create a new chamber of Kung Fu mastery. The elder monk says if you can master our highest chamber, you can develop your own. The young monk, in all of his ambition, convinced the elder to allow him to start with the last chamber. He was expecting to experience an advanced fighting style therein; instead, he found a room full of meditating monks, sitting still. He could not handle the psychic energy of stillness and begged to go back to the beginning. In the following pages, we will detail for you several tips and practical steps that can be taken in order to approach the experience of stillness, without losing your mind. With enough practice, you should be able to manifest a peaceful, still state of mind and body, whenever you will it to be.

1. Honor Presence and Intention

Part of keeping still is the refusal to be distracted by those things that detract from your ability to be well, and to be productive. By acknowledging your own presence, as well as that of others, along with setting intentions for everything that you do, you will decrease the element of scatter that often comes with haphazard movements and an aloof perspective. Guarding your time from distracting elements is a solid first step towards being still.

2. Attend to Your Inner Peace

Daily exercise, deep breathing, yoga, affirmations, and mantras are various ways to keep you connected with inner stillness. Being able to situate yourself in these moments helps to bring about clarity during tough situations as you engage students, interact with colleagues, and attempt to partner with parents. It is often easier to prevent a situation from escalating through a calming presence, than it is to deescalate a situation that has already gotten out of hand. Focus on developing an inner balance through meditation. This brings us closer to having an outer clarity and more solid base from which to act. Turning inward decreases the amount of energy dissipated by an outward focus, thereby providing a more purposeful engagement with life.

3. Rise in the Morning Earlier Than You Need To

Giving yourself time in the morning to wake up and simply be, provides a much needed and most beneficial transition point for starting your day. If you use an alarm, set it 15 minutes earlier than when you would typically set it. Eventually you want to trust your own awareness of time so you will no longer need an alarm, but until then, try to find the most gentle alert to ease you awake. Once you have awakened, take a moment to just lay there and express gratitude for another opportunity to do and be better. Program your day by visualizing how you want it to unfold. Once you have done this, calmly get out of bed and set about your day feeling confident that your intentions have been set, and will manifest.

4. Take a Little Time Between Tasks to Re-Center Yourself

Often times we seamlessly go from one activity or engagement to the next. This is how people make mistakes, and eventually experience burn-out. We know that burnout is very taxing on our health (mental and physical) and negatively impacts our productivity. By intentionally pausing between tasks for the purpose of "collecting yourself," you are increasing the likelihood of performing each task optimally, and giving yourself a much needed mini-respite.

5. Incorporate Stillness into Your Classroom Routine with Students

The educator who implements this tip within their classroom routine is the educator that brings a certain level of solace and serenity to their students and work environment. We have literally seen classrooms transformed by simply having students take ten deep breaths upon finishing an assignment, and before moving on to the next. "Stillness competitions" are a fun and effective way of getting children to sit still for a few moments. This is done by rewarding the group who can sit still and quiet the longest, within a one-minute period. By bringing your own stillness into the classroom, you will surely set the tone for those under your care. Lead by example.

Self-Care Tip #5

SELF-AWARENESS

Self-awareness is one of the most valuable tools to develop, regardless of profession and life circumstance. Self-awareness, as an instrument for self-care, affords us the ability to distinguish between our personal "stuff" and the "stuff" of others. It awakens in the self-aware educator, the ability to self-monitor, which then allows us to recognize when we are functioning in balance or operating in imbalance.

This tool is necessary if we are to truly understand how we contribute to the situations in which we find ourselves. Without self-awareness, we can easily find ourselves in the bottomless pit of shifting the blame. As an educator, lacking in self-awareness, we can easily become enmeshed with the emotions, dramas, and personal situations of our co-workers, the children in our care, and even their families. This enmeshed state usually occurs because we are not clear about whose feelings and thoughts we are experiencing. And sometimes, we are simply unaware of the motivation behind our own thoughts and feelings.

As a concrete example, think about the last time you met a rude person (a clerk at the supermarket or a waitress at your local restaurant), and found your self

> **Self-Awareness And Self-Monitoring Allow You To Discern YOUR Stuff From Everyone Else's Stuff**

in a bad mood as a result of the experience you had with them. You may be totally unaware of why you have suddenly become upset. It is also unlikely that you understand that you have actually taken on the emotions of the other person, claiming it as your own. The hidden danger in this experience is not only the fact that negative emotions are known to have detrimental psychological and physiological effects, but also because of the likelihood that you will begin to act out of, and treat others based on, this emotional transference.

Self-awareness goes beyond knowing how you are feeling and being able to distinguish between your emotions and psychological state, and that of another with whom you are interacting. It also includes the ability to read yourself similar to how a barometer reads atmospheric pressure, or how the "pre-collision assist technology," found in newer cars, scans the road and helps to prevent accidents. Imagine being able to see when your emotional "peace and calm" are being threatened long before reaching a critical state. Imagine being able to know the situations that typically cause you the most angst in life, and instead of avoiding them, you approach them with confidence and a sense of self-mastery.

Having self-awareness as an educator is the gateway to becoming more efficient and effective. It allows for a sense of empathy that is more clear, and therefore more accurate, when it comes to having understanding for your colleagues and students. Being a self-aware educator helps in the process of unpacking personal baggage, which then frees us from making unnecessary mistakes and bad calls when solving problems. It makes us less likely to confuse our personal views, desires, and opinions with the "best decision" for the situations we often face. In other words, we are more fully capable of exercising objectivity when it comes to decision making.

The notion of self-awareness is not the same as being critical of one's actions, beliefs, and thoughts. On the contrary, this concept is more about being observant of our personal idiosyncrasies as we move about our daily lives. It's about being fully capable of making a swift and accurate assessment of ourselves, and rendering appropriate judgment on what we find. I know, we are supposed to live non-judgmental lives, right? Wrong. It is virtually impossible for us to live a life without judgment. In fact, everything that you do involves making some sort of a judgment call. For instance, in order for you to sit down in a chair, you will have to assess and determine (judge) how far away that chair actually is in order to use the appropriate amount of leg strength to lower you the proper distance. Without this, you will likely hit the chair too hard, and suffer for it.

Likewise, we are judging others every time we choose to engage or not engage people we encounter. This too, is perfectly okay. In fact, we are biologically designed to judge as a means for survival. The notion of living a non-judgmental life is sort of a knee-jerk reaction to the desire to not be negatively judged based on stereotypes. Saying and understanding it this way allows for a better, more truthful understanding of the power and inevitability of making judgments throughout life. We are more prone to err, when we are incapable of distinguishing our "stuff" from that of another.

The following points are designed to get you started on your quest to becoming more aware of yourself, and then taking this newfound awareness and appropriately applying it to your craft as an educator. By this point in the guide, you should be keenly aware of how these tips naturally intersect with one another, and you should be able to start applying points and insights from other sections to the ones you are currently working on.

Be
Still

Meditation

Physical
Well-Being

Unify With
Like Minds

1. Unapologetically Pursue Self-Knowledge

"You are the ONLY version of you in ALL of existence, why not be the best?" This, and the millions of other quotable clichés, sound good to the ear, but what do they really mean? How do they look when put into practice? In this case, we would first have to get to know ourselves, understanding that each of us consist of a very complex set of elements from both nature and our nurturing. Pay special attention to personal desires, take a few personality tests, and ask the people that knew you as a child to describe your characteristics. Seek both the "good" aspects of your personality, as well as the Shadow, and understand there are strengths and weaknesses in both. Set as a goal for yourself, the full integration of all aspects of you as a person. Face your fears and those not-so-pleasant traits, refine and integrate them into your daily walk.

2. Seek Truth

The famous adage that "the truth shall make you free" is poignant and necessary as we seek to raise awareness in order to bring about peace within ourselves, and our teaching environments. Truth, as it relates to our own shortcomings, can allow for swift refinement and development. The more we deal with the truth within ourselves, relationships, and professional lives, the easier it will be to enact positive change and achieve health and well-being. Be honest with yourself! The truth brings you face to face with humanity and will be what it is, whether or not you believe it, see it, or understand it. A most beneficial by-product of seeking and living the truth is the ability to discern the truth from falsehood. This keen level of discernment can't be bought or taught. It must be earned by first becoming so familiar and acclimated to the truth, that anything that is not the truth, becomes obvious.

3. Prioritize Self-Refinement

Almost everyone is susceptible to "peer pressure." Even as adults, we have to negotiate our existence based on how those we care about will view our desires, actions, decisions, and motivations. Frustration in life comes most often to those who resent doing or not doing something simply because it may or may not have been "approved" by another. Within this category, the most costly are those where we had opportunities to improve upon ourselves and we didn't. As educators, we bring ourselves to our jobs whether we know it or not. It is through our condition that all lessons are passed along to our students, colleagues, and staff. If you are raggedy (on the inside), then something about your performance will reflect that. For this reason, It is super important for us to make our personal growth and development, by way of refinement, a priority in life. Remember, the better you are, the better you show up.

4. Embrace the Pivot

Along the road to refinement we are likely to encounter situations that call for us to choose a different route. For many, these moments highlight our own vulnerabilities as it usually requires us to admit a flaw in our thinking or approach. As school and classroom leaders, these moments typically bring our judgment and intellect into question. Remember, making mistakes is normal and the wisdom gained from those mistakes only strengthen us as educators. When you find yourself needing to pivot, it is time to embrace the lesson and allow yourself to find peace through the process. On the other side of vulnerability is courage; being a living example of this, will ultimately allow you to connect deeply with yourself and build lasting relationships with others. It is never too late to make adjustments and make amends; in fact, these are often positive signs of intentional growth and development.

Self-Care Tip #6

BE CREATIVE

Creativity expresses itself infinitely throughout the entire universe. It is everywhere and in all things including you! The human experience is filled with creative moments and the opportunity we have to express this creative force, intentionally, is nothing short of a miracle. Purposely positioning yourself inside these moments is the path towards living and being part of the ongoing, never-ending creative process. Remember, we always have a choice: Do you tap into to your creative potential, or do you squander the opportunity and waste the resource? Will I take this five minutes to sit still and breathe, creatively visualizing my desired outcome before going into this interview, or will I give in to nervousness and miss this opportunity to take life by the reins? Will I take the first few moments after waking up to scroll through social media, or will I use that time to apply my creative intentions to plan my day?

Our lives are replete with daily glimpses of insight, moments of truth, and spaces of revelation and truth seeking. However, we still look outside of ourselves for creative inspiration, which seems perfectly natural as we experience the outside world.

> Begin By Asking Yourself, "How Can I Shift My Creative Vision From a Noun To a Verb?"

This is perfectly okay because our external world is marvelous and full of inspiration. What we are hoping to highlight in this part of the guide is how all of these external experiences impacting our lives, are directly connected to our inner selves. And how we, by tapping into the inner-flow of creativity, can begin to bring our internal and external worlds into harmony, granting us a disposition that is both powerful and soothing to those fortunate enough to experience it. We are hereby offering to you, within the pages of this guide, a blueprint of sorts, designed to empower and sustain you in the greatness that is you.

As human beings, we are able to actualize our creative potential by bringing it into our personal spaces and professional practice. In order to intentionally do this, our creative awareness must be as ubiquitous to us as the air we breathe. When combined with our tips for being still, developing self-awareness, and meditation, we open ourselves to a deeper level of self-knowledge, which is the key to all knowledge.

The longer you live, the more you will notice that life provides ample opportunities to show and prove what you claim to know. Actualizing and carrying the tips in this guide with you each and every day, is a surefire way to be prepared to pass these universal "tests." Wait, are you saying that the universe will test us? Yup! Have you ever declared that you would no longer eat something, then all of a sudden you are provided ample opportunities to eat it? Like suddenly someone brings you a Costco sized bag of that very candy bar you gave up for Lent or as part of your New Year's resolution? This is the universe providing you an opportunity to prove, to yourself, that you are serious. Creatively and symbolically visualizing your steadfastness in the face of these tests is one of the best ways to succeed.

So how do we operationalize this creative energy? Let's look into one of the first things that teachers and administrators do when beginning a new school year: we return to our "space" and seek to personalize and decorate our work environments to reflect our intentions for the upcoming year. This is true whether it is a luxurious office, a classroom, a desk in the corner, a cubby, or locker; no matter how big or small, we should respect the power in our ability to create. As we go about this annual ritual, there are a number of savvy ways to transform the mundane into something magical! The key is to intentionally use your creativity to shape, mold, and influence your environment in order to produce specific results: an environment conducive to learning.

Your meditation practice and the resulting wisdom can and should be with you at all times. You cannot afford to wait until you reach home; our responsibilities as educators and school leaders demand that we are flexible and can tap into a state of stillness even while engaging an enraged parent or clueless board member, tweaking an impossible budget, or supporting an anxious child. This level of stealthy fierceness is accomplished through intentional practice. How you choose to approach it is a function of your own creativity.

Being able to visualize yourself at peace, in perfect health, or engaging in rational decision-making, is a superior way to access this state and making it a reality. Begin by asking yourself, "How can I shift my creative vision from a noun to a verb?" What symbolic representation can you bring into your work space to trigger feelings of health and peace of mind? How creative can you be in using simple items to represent complex desires and states of being? Seek to imbue everyday items with reverence and personal power. This will totally change your perspective of what it means to be empowered, and how far you can take your creative nature.

Below are a few tips to further guide you in the use of your creative energies. You have everything necessary to be successful, now it is time to use these gifts and talents with more intention, more confidence, and more awareness.

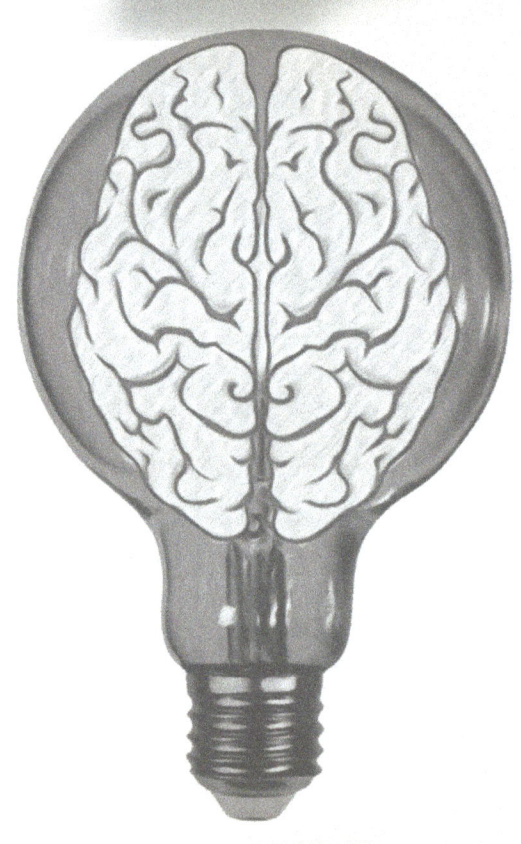

1. Use Creative Visualization to Manifest Goals & Aspirations

As children, it was normal for us to use our imaginations and to fantasize about how we wanted things to be. Believe it or not, that childhood past-time is actually a powerful tool we can use as adults to bring changes to our professional and personal lives. Spend several minutes each morning envisioning a great and blessed day for yourself and watch your experiences begin to shift. See the end result of what you desire, in as much detail as possible, until you are able to experience it as a real and tangible event.

2. Use Symbols to Represent Ideas

Using symbols is a way to reduce complex ideas into manageable chunks. Symbols provide an efficient way to convey and memorize information, thereby freeing up mental resources for doing other work. Symbols are also easy to infuse into your everyday environments. For example, if you are focused on getting a promotion, you can symbolically represent this as someone climbing a mountain and place that picture at your desk or on the wall in your classroom. To most, it will just be art, to you, it is a constant reminder, motivator, and focal point.

3. Envision Your Creativity

A vision board (VB) is a great means for gathering your symbolic representations into one shared space. A VB can be crafted to represent a flow chart of how you will achieve certain goals. It can also be developed to represent the "end game," as it relates to how you'd like to position yourself professionally. Vision boards can even be used as tools to acknowledge and show gratitude for one's current life experiences. Whatever the purpose, your VB should have a positive impact on your emotions, and should wed the desired goals to the good feelings generated by the symbolic imagery used. With modern technology, VBs have become infinitely more creative and definitely more transferable and accessible. At one time we had to get poster boards and magazines for "cut and paste parties." Now, we can simply search the Internet for pictures and create collages. These can then be used as screen savers, background images, and even transferred onto canvas, clothing, or simply projected onto a wall at home or work. Consider creating vision boards with your class and/or colleagues. See how powerful this tool is at re-centering and focusing your students on their collective and individual goals.

4. Develop Confidence in Your Ability to Be Creative

Unfortunately, as we grow older, many of us become less and less creative. We begin to fall into a routine of how things get done. We feel that we have less and less time to do things and therefore we begin to see everyday tasks as a burden. One way to avoid falling into this trap is to remain creative and expressive. This is often most easily accomplished by taking on a hobby that involves designing and making new items, or improvements to old ones. Having confidence in your ability to create something valuable is the key to stepping up your creativity.

5. Take Time to Write Things Out

Handwriting is slowly becoming a lost art. It's known that we remember things better when we take handwritten notes. It is also known that writing helps our minds to process thoughts and experiences, thereby alleviating certain burdens associated with mental and emotional baggage. This can be done by what we call "creative journaling." This is a form of writing where you write about whatever comes to mind. We suggest getting a dedicated notebook, and allowing yourself at least 15 minutes per day to enjoy this exercise. It carries a similar benefit to some forms of talk therapy.

Self-Care Tip #7

BE PRODUCTIVE

When speaking of being productive, we are talking about more than the efficient use of time, in order to maximize output and meeting our job-related goals. In this tip, we are also referencing the idea of productivity that includes the manufacturing of a tangible product that in some way or another, enhances you personally, and has a beneficial impact on the lives others. The process of producing draws heavily on our ability to be creative, confident, driven, resourceful, empowered, and unapologetic. This means that by pushing ourselves to produce a product, we are by default developing the aforementioned traits and characteristics along the way.

The product that we produce does not have to be something marketable, and it does not necessarily have to be something that we directly share with others. It can simply be a project, a product of our hobby; something that requires us to push through internal roadblocks, insecurities, and stagnation. In other words, growing towards productivity requires us to shift our mode of functioning from that of a passive consumer and observer of life, to one that applies creativity with the intention of

> Being Productive Is More Than The Efficient Use Of Time. It Involves The Manifestation Of Thoughts And Ideas. It's The Product Of Your Creativity.

bringing ideas to full manifestation. The first product is typically the most difficult because it requires us to take the largest leap. The subsequent products tend to flow easier because the process has been demystified and proven doable.

By increasing your productivity, you are also increasing your aptitude for creativity. The two go hand-in-hand. As a producer, you become a more efficient and effective thinker because you have trained your brain to see into the future, anticipating needs and problems that may arise based on your desired end-product. This is where the saying "Chess Not Checkers" comes into play. Simple products are a great place to start, but it is important to increase the complexity of your ideas, methods, and final products if you are to continue to grow and benefit from being a productive agent in society.

Existing in a productive head-space is facilitated by the ability to think clearly. The skills and tools acquired by following Tip #1, meditation, will benefit you greatly when it comes to gaining command over your productive capabilities. Many people find that they work best when their environment is clean and clear vs. cluttered and confusing, however keep in mind that one person's clutter is another person's system. Knowing this allows you to accept your means of cultivating creativity and productivity, without falling into the frustration of trying to accept and conform to what others have done for themselves. Models are a good and valuable source of inspiration, just remember that you are free to add your own creative elements to their suggestions and methods, or reject them altogether.

Some judge the quality of your productivity to be the external manifestation of what is happening on the inside. Interestingly, by being productive, you are also shaping and refining your inner world; it is a bi-directional and reciprocal relationship. Being a producer, whether it be of ideas, art, music, stories, clothing, etc., is one of the many ways we use our inner vision to engage the world around us. Producing thoughtful solutions to problems within your school or personal life, helps to feed your sense of purpose. In your producer mode, you are likely to develop and stick to plans, which in turn, encourages timeliness. Doing things in a timely and efficient manner, and being able to complete tasks and meet goals & objectives ahead of schedule, will free up your time, and thereby provide you with a greater window of opportunity to enhance your personal life. Productivity, in this regard, also serves to alleviate the stress of always feeling pressured by time and deadlines related to externally determined obligations.

On a more philosophical level, being productive puts us in line with other aspects of nature, which are constantly providing a product that directly benefits other forms of creation (i.e., plants are constantly producing oxygen for aerobic lifeforms to inhale). Sharing your talents with the world, and receiving the passionate creations of others, is what makes humans naturally interdependent. Producing from our own creativity can provide some of the most profound opportunities to connect and collaborate with others on a deeper, more genuine level. The following points are developed to encourage and motivate you to take the necessary steps towards become a producer of things that are beneficial to others. This should be done while simultaneously improving your efficiency and effectiveness when it comes to meeting goals and objectives. These are two sides of the same coin, meaning you can't develop one without improving the other.

Have A Hobby

Creativity

Meditation

Professional Development

1. Acknowledge Your Productivity Highs and Lows

This self-awareness exercise allows you to evaluate your propensity for being productive. By taking an objective view of your personal performance at work, at home, and in social contexts, you can begin to acknowledge those things that motivate and encourage you, as well as those things that stifle and dampen your soul. This information is vital when it comes to developing plans and working towards goals. You will also benefit from identifying all of the things you have ever produced in life, whether it be a child, an idea, a concept, a song, a handshake, whatever. If you have created it, count it and explore ways you can build upon it.

2. Have Patience with Yourself

We can sometimes be abusive and harsh to ourselves; more harsh than anyone else. This experience is usually related to a sense of frustration, and will only grow if overlooked or intentionally ignored. Failure to accomplish goals and/or a failure to even try, are the usual culprits creating this negative disposition. We tend to be most vulnerable to negative self-talk, and have less patience with ourselves when we are feeling stagnant and unproductive. This becomes a self-propelling cycle because the negative feelings actually fuel the lack of productivity, which then makes it less likely that we will be productive. This may be a time when more internalized reflection is needed in order to bring you out of the slumps, and into higher levels of productivity.

3. Identify and Respect Your Creative Cycle

Determine the best time of day, the best season, and the ideal space for you to be most productive. Take the time to figure yourself out, so that you are able to have control over your output. Understand that productivity does not always equate to physical manifestations; it could refer to producing ideas and concepts, or mental symbols for use in your creative visualizations and meditations. Honor where you are in your own pattern of productivity and understand that it may look very different from others. Seek to identify those things that contribute to, and hinder, your productivity.

4. Know What Systems of Organization Work Best for You

Explore taking voice recorded memos to serve as notes or utilizing a tried and true calendar system so that you aren't missing important appointments or opportunities. Sometimes what we need is structure or a set routine to get our productivity flowing. There exists an interesting relationship between creativity and productivity. Some of our most creative and imaginative minds have a difficult time bringing their thoughts into reality, while some of our most productive people, those with the drive to do, function best when someone else gives them the idea and/or blueprint. Then there are those who have worked on themselves and have enhanced both aspects within their own person.

5. Stay Fueled and Energized

Keep high vibration food on your plate and avoid foods that make you "sleepy" after you eat them. This is definitely counter-productive, and forces you to fight an uphill battle against an undefeated force, sleep.

Self-Care Tip #8

UNITE LIKE-MINDS

We live in an individualistic, fast-paced world that favors technology over face-to-face interactions, and device-mediated relationships rather than having intimate and meaningful in-person contact. Educators, now more than ever, must make a concerted effort to seek out and nurture authentic relationships, especially because of the tendency to form superficial, social media-based connections. Even in the world of cyberspace, we are capable of, and should prioritize our need to unite with like minds. This is done by joining education-related groups, and by following those who offer great educational advice that is also practically applicable. Maybe consider forming your own group, or develop a page where you are the one moderating discussions and sharing/posting education related information. This ensures that you are not only learning from others, but also learning from your own research and provision of information to your "tribe."

Building trust and camaraderie with colleagues is an extremely vital part of creating a healthy support system. These types of intentional and positive networks help to bring about peace of mind and a sense of solidarity when faced with adversity both

> Tap Into The Power Of Affinity Groups And Thought Partnership With Like-minded People.
> Make The Connection.
> Seek Out Opportunities To Gather Wisdom And Share Insights.

on the job, and in our personal lives. This does not require us to agree with everything stated and/or done by our co-workers, but it does require that we maintain a clear understanding of our common goal and singular purpose when it comes to providing stellar educational experiences to our students. If we all agree to this as our goal, the "what" and "how" of it all becomes more objectively measurable, and less burdensome because there is less opposition to the core concept.

Being part of a like-minded community also provides a sense of belonging, which itself provides confidence and nurturing to the membership. This is a foundational human need, and serves as an instrumental factor in healthy social development. By seeking out those who share similar interests and/or who have an overall affinity for those things that you consider important and life affirming, you are on your way to finding your oasis in the desert.

Having a tribe does not mean becoming part of a monolithic group of people. On the contrary, it's about merging with the various and diverse pieces of your professional and personal puzzle; each component playing its part for the whole, while expressing itself as a unique and autonomous manifestation. The strength of this thought-partnership, with people from different backgrounds and worldviews, is found in the varied but unified approach to common goals. This union can assist with the broadening of your understanding and perspective, which is a sure indication that you are engaged in true learning and true empowerment.

Regarding our emotional health and well-being, having a group of like-minded people to speak with on a professional level, can provide a safe place for emotional release. Having other professionals that can relate to you and your experience of hardship is cathartic. Being able to vent, without feeling the need to overly explain your feelings and perspective, is an invaluably rare privilege in today's workplace. Also found amongst like-minded colleagues, are objective perspectives that can offer criticism without the sting and uncertainty that may occur when it comes from a source culturally-distant from your own.

It is important to note and understand the difference between venting and perspective taking. There are certainly times when releasing strong emotions in a safe space is beneficial both mentally and physically, this is venting. During these times you may also find that you're not in the best place to receive and hear advice. This is okay, and is a normal part of the process. In many cases, we need to "get things off our chest" before we are receptive enough to take advice from another. Once relieved of the emotional burden, we can advance to the stage of personal accountability. This is where having an accountability partner, one who has permission to point out our flaws, and to nudge us toward self-awareness and reflection, comes in handy. With this, we are in a space that is supportive of deeper thinking, and that facilitates our reaching higher for overall understanding and peace of mind. Keep in mind that the friend or colleagues you vent to, are not necessarily those from whom you take perspective. Knowing the difference between these two and not having high expectations of finding sound resolution during the moments of intense release is wisdom.

As with the other tips, take a moment to read and reflect on the following imagery and listing of ideas related to uniting with like minds. Remember, you are building personal networks that are designed to meet your basic human need for social interaction, while simultaneously supporting your professional endeavors.

1. Seek Encouraging Friendships

It is beneficial to have a core group of friends or family members who provide strong encouragement and support during challenging times. This is not always available within your immediate professional circle because people are often competitive towards co-workers and professional colleagues. For example, it can be difficult for a qualified educator who is seeking the "Head of School" position, to receive support from fellow teachers who may be thinking about their "peer" becoming their "boss," and receiving a significant increase in pay. Professional colleagues from outside of the immediate circle will likely be free of those issues, and therefore can, and likely will, be more supportive.

2. Join Critical Friends and Professional Learning Circles

These spaces provide varying levels of professional support amongst like-minded educators, with whom you share professional interests and/or personal affinities. Seek these out through your school, regional professional association, or even online. Here is where you can gain professional insights; information that leads directly to you performing your job more efficiently and effectively. A coalition of middle school Montessori teachers is an excellent example of such a group. Here you will find teachers with very similar duties and responsibilities, and who are able to provide a wealth of information, insight, and tips for improving your value, contribution, competence, and confidence.

3. Understanding the Village Concept

No person is an island, no one stands alone. Finding alignment within intentional spaces that also support and challenge you is necessary. Our society pushes a narrative that emphasizes the "I." However, the majority of people on the planet are from collectivist cultures that actually affirm the "We." When you deliberately situate yourself in a community of people, take on an agreed upon role that will assure its survival, and dedicate yourself to making sure that whoever needs help gets helped the most. You are now living the Village mentality. This Concept has a direct impact on our mental health and supports us as we strive to derive meaning from a world that may often seem confusing. As school leaders, we often find solace and strength in understanding our roles and seeing positive outcomes first-hand. Our schools, in many ways, become our village, and caring for the members of our community is a way to ensure that the good outweighs the bad. Recognizing that our schools are dynamic systems built upon the interdependence and interrelatedness of a group of people, provides a powerful perspective of how our individual roles combine to serve the whole.

4. Push Against Feelings of Discomfort When Around "Others"

While we should never apologize for finding comfort amongst "our own," it is also a sign of growth and development when we can power-through this comfort zone and explore experiences with others. What often happens, and has been demonstrated on numerous occasions, is that we find more in common with others than we previously thought possible, and derive great benefit from the differences they bring.

Self-Care Tip #9

HAVE A HOBBY

For the most part, hobbies are enjoyable outlets people tend to take on voluntarily. They are often low-pressure activities that are free from externally imposed values, requirements, judgments, and binding input. For some, hobbies serve as a vacation from all the obligatory aspects of life. In this same light, hobbies can also provide an invigorating challenge to the hobbyist, pushing them beyond comfort zones and the stagnating and repetitious nature of the work-a-day life. What specific value does having a hobby bring to the life of an educator?

Hobbies can provide a respite for the educator's mind. This is done by giving the mind something other than students, lesson plans, and work related drama to focus on, and by drawing on the tips and information highlighted in the areas of creativity and productivity. When combined, this triune of self-expression is the perfect remedy for boredom, complacency, lethargy, depression, and other warning signs of burnout and educator fatigue.

We are all multifaceted beings, who, without a proper means of expression, can be reduced to a unidimensional, flattened version of our potential greatness.

> Having A Hobby Is A Fun And Creative Way To Sharpen Existing Skills, And A Great Way To Develop New Ones

This is a guaranteed formula for frustration and a feeling of worthlessness, and potential resentment towards the profession. Being forced into a limited mode of expression not only hinders the one being limited, but also robs the environment of the greater potential they have to offer. This limiting effect is not like the one mentioned in the section on establishing boundaries, mainly because these limitations are often being externally imposed upon us, in an oppressive and negatively controlling manner. Expressing oneself by way of a hobby, allows educators the freedom to share more of themselves with the world, while simultaneously growing and learning more about what it is they have to offer. It is the perfect counter-balance to the aforementioned restrictions.

This tip finds its value and importance amongst educators because we tend to be super dedicated to our job and profession, and oft-times are willing to sacrifice the best parts of ourselves for the future we are responsible for molding, namely our students. Amidst all of this, we must find ways to feed and express the other sides of ourselves. Channeling creativity towards a hobby totally unrelated to your job may be just the thing you need to make connections, build a restorative outlet, and learn even more about yourself and the otherwise hidden aspects of your life. The more you get out to explore and discover things that make you tick, the better you will show up and show out in the classroom!

Let's say, for example, you have an interest in making rock climbing a hobby and therefore decide to join a rock climbing club. This move will not only allow you to associate with others of like minds and similar interests, but will also develop your confidence and physical well-being. This almost guarantees that you will be more energetic in the classroom, more courageous and confident in presenting your lessons, and in overall better shape as a result. Talk about getting it in!!!

Or, let's say you like to explore fashion as a hobby. Perhaps you had a dream and desire to become a fashion designer or fashion model in a previous life (before becoming a teacher/administrator). There is nothing preventing you from taking this up as a hobby while also being an educator. This can be done by keeping up with trending designers, creatively developing your own style (which I am sure you already have by way of your daily swag), and perhaps, by signing up for workshops on sewing and design. This will enhance your creativity, provide you an outlet for creative expression, and perhaps provide you with a product for sale or "show-and-tell."

Hobbies provide us with outlets and skill building experiences, which can be put into practice right there in the classroom. I know, you're thinking your worlds are colliding because hobbies are supposed to take us away from our day-to-day work routine. True enough, but because nothing is ever really separate, we can benefit from finding creative ways to intentionally link things together. Our fashionista teacher, for example, can develop a fashion show with their students as models. Or our rock-climbing teacher could start a "bouldering club," striking up a partnership with the local climbing gym and getting parents involved. Both hobbies would serve as an excellent fundraising opportunity for the school, and would definitely be a lot of fun for all parties involved. Remember, whenever you are directly improving yourself, you are enhancing how you show up in all aspects of your life, including work. Leave your mark of greatness for others to enjoy.

The following points will give you a bit more direction on how to employ this tip, and make the most out of having a hobby. Take your time and really incorporate the principles from previous and related tips in order to maximize the benefits from your endeavors.

Be Productive

Meditation

Creativity

Unify With Like Minds

1. Choose a Hobby that You Truly Enjoy

What good is a hobby if you don't really find pleasure in it. Why choose to do something that is less than exciting as your form of creative release? Choosing a hobby should be taken seriously, and is likely not that difficult once we slow down enough to pay attention and remember what we actually find pleasure in. It is highly likely that you are already participating in your hobby in some form or another. It could be the case that you simply have to make it official by declaring it as such. Making it official provides perspective and intentionality to your extra-curricular activities, which is healing to the soul and can prove beneficial to our overall well-being.

2. See Your Hobby as an Opportunity for Self-Care

Understanding that your hobby is a great source of stress-relief, a means to build mental fortitude, and for developing yourself in a holistic manner, can deepen the value you ascribe to the activity. Using hobbies as a form of self-care unofficially happens all the time. Many of us have "that thing" we do to relieve our stress or forget about the busy-busy parts of life. Making it official, and declaring our hobbies to be a valuable source for self-care will elevate how we both value and appreciate the moments spent in that space. So rather than blindly running to your hobby for relief while in the midst of crisis, try easing into it consistently and outside of the high-stress context. Make a commitment to yourself by committing to your hobby as a form of self-care.

3. Find A Consistent Time & Space to Engage Your Hobby

Making your hobby a habit is important. An activity becomes habitual once we no longer have to think about doing it; once we are on autopilot. Habits have a way of making themselves known by creating a craving within us that is difficult, if not impossible to resist. Being consistent with our hobbies will help to transform them from a thing we plan to do, into the thing that we are willfully compelled to do. Because our habits are healthy, we won't concern ourselves with the imbalances often associated with negative habits like drug addiction. Having a healthy habitual hobby should become your mission as you seek to identify and develop self-care activities for yourself.

4. Find a Hobby that Requires You to Develop New Skills

Part of the value of having a hobby is the opportunity to learn and stretch your mind. We often get into a mode where we repeatedly exercise the same parts of the brain, in the exact same way, which rarely produces any new connections. By engaging a hobby that is both challenging and desirable, we gain an opportunity to enhance ourselves on a cognitive level. For those who are naturally "left-brain-oriented," constantly doing intellectual things, it is highly recommended that you find a hobby that relaxes your left hemisphere while activating your artistically-expressive right hemisphere. If you have an affinity for so-called "right-brained" activities, seek to embrace the sometimes unattractive activities that enhance and engage your left hemisphere (i.e., logic puzzles). "Left-brainers" can choose music production, graphic design, and other forms of artistic expression as hobbies to achieve that much need escape from their intellectual day-to-day lives.

Self-Care Tip #10

PROFESSIONAL DEVELOPMENT

Empowered teachers are those who take responsibility for their continued growth and development on both the professional and personal levels. One way this is achieved is by actively seeking out professional development opportunities that are not only designed to expand your craft as an educator, but that are also aligned with your personal interests and passions. This blend may seem to be an impossible combination; but in reality, it only takes a bit of self-reflection and creativity to see that it is more than possible, it is actually probable.

Professional development typically occurs in one of two ways: on-site or off-site. In the on-site experience, an expert is either selected from amongst the existing staff, or someone is brought in to present on an area of need and/or interest. This process is typically initiated or at least directed by administrative staff. These are more common because they are cost effective and allow for a standardizing of the education received by the staff. By exposing the majority of their staff to one training, administrators are not dependent upon a few staff members to "bring back" their knowledge and experiences from an off-site conference or workshop. The fact that everyone receives the

> Developing Your Professional Competence Enhances Your Confidence In Other Aspects Of Life.

exact same information at the same time, in the same context, allows for continuity of discussion and a seamless building upon the ideas offered by the instructor.

On the other hand, off-site PDs can offer more of a variety and can tailor more readily to the interests of those fortunate enough to attend. Educators attending off-site professional development opportunities have the freedom and flexibility to select those experiences that speak directly to their needs and interests, especially if they are attending a large conference with a variety of workshops and speakers. The downside to this option is that it can be very costly, and therefore, limited to only a relatively small number of people. For those living in major metropolitan areas such as Washington, DC, there is a unique advantage because large education conferences are frequently hosted in these locales, which makes it easier on the pockets for larger numbers of school staff to attend (because travel and lodging costs are eliminated). There are also more local organizations in these areas that sponsor PD opportunities at little to no cost.

Take a moment to think about the last professional development you attended. Was it something that was brought to your campus by administration? If so, was it actually facilitated and conducted by a co-worker? What kind of input did you have? What kinds of feedback did you offer? Was it off-site? How did you maximize the opportunity? Were you there on a mission to "find your tribe" as mentioned in tip #8? Or were you there on a reconnaissance mission, seeking to bring back as much as possible to your fellow front-line teaching warriors? Of course many of us likely prefer the option to go off-site for our trainings. Few things are better than getting out of the classroom and living in a hotel room for a few days while basking in intellectually stimulating, and practically applicable bliss...not to mention the opportunity to trade war stories at the bar in the lobby with your newly found family of educators. Believe it or not, there is an approach to PD that brings us the best of both worlds.

As an educator, you should make it your mission to uplift your co-workers by way of enhancing their knowledge, skills, and competencies. For those of us that are more proactive in seeking out PDs to attend off-site, it is incumbent upon us to find those experts that we can bring back to campus to share the wealth. This not only benefits our school, but it also provides an opportunity to the educator coming to conduct the training. This creates a win-win situation.

So far we have spoken on how PDs assist in raising our job-related skills for direct application at our current schools, in our current role. It may come as no surprise to some of you that there is also a more "selfish" motivation behind our pursuit of PDs, that is, the development of you as an individual. By engaging in as much training and development as possible, we enhance our status as an asset to our institution. This will help to build confidence in our self-concept, which works to increase the value we ascribe to ourselves as educators. This comes in handy especially for those of us who feel that we are often overlooked for in-house promotions and other opportunities. When we know our value, we don't take those "slights" personally; instead, we see it as an opportunity to get out there and see what others may have to offer. We call this "walk-away-power."

It is both valuable and important to seek out opportunities that assist in reaching personal and professional goals, and that speak directly to your interests and passions. Thinking outside the box will ensure that you are open to diverse experiences and approaches to content. Push the envelope and get out of your comfort zone. Build your professional acumen, grow deeper in your understanding of self, and make sure you honor what you bring to your organization and your students. Take the following tips as your guide for seeking out and enjoying professional development experiences.

1. Find Opportunities that Stretch Your Thinking and Perspective

Always strive to put yourself in professional spaces that push you to think deeper and prepare you for future endeavors. A major goal of your quest for professional development opportunities should be to expand your understanding and perspective as it relates to your duties and responsibilities as an educator. Your professional development opportunities should drive you to dig deeper into the information you already "know," and should encourage you to seek and develop a keener understanding of the subject at hand.

2. Seek Opportunities that are Exciting and Interactive

Few things are worse than a boring professional development activity. While all of them aren't likely to be a party in disguise, you should strive to participate in those that are at least engaging. As educators, we know very well that a variety of learning styles exist within any group of students, and that we do best in reaching them by providing a variety of teaching styles for the same subject. This remains true for us as adult students. Check in with others regarding specific trainers and PD opportunities before signing up. Inquire about their style, level of engagement, and even their personality. If you ever attend one of our sessions, you will find yourself being thoroughly engaged, and perhaps even entertained (usually by corny jokes, and insightful analogies). The more you are moving and engaging in fun ways, the more likely the content will stick and become part of your professional practice.

3. See Professional Development as Personal Development

Understanding that your Professional Development opportunities are also opportunities for personal development will greatly assist you in selecting those with more value and life enhancing qualities. You should be ever on a mission to retool yourself; constantly evolving in your craft and ever ready to take on the next opportunity that is just outside of the range of your current duties and responsibilities. By staying sharp and on your toes, you will likely gain more appreciation and a sense of being valued from your existing administration. Few things motivate a stagnate administration, that takes their best and brightest employees for granted, than a phone call from an organization ready to hire you.

4. Proactively Seek Opportunities

Teachers should not depend on administrators to find and provide them with options; instead, actively seek them out on your own. Bring ideas to the table and share them with your co-workers. If you are an administrator, encourage your staff to seek out and bring back such opportunities. This will serve the purpose of providing variety, while also strengthening the voice of your staff. Identifying unique experiences that teachers find relevant and easy to implement can be challenging for school administrators. This approach helps to eliminate or at least address that concern. By empowering yourself and your staff, you enhance the opportunities available to the families and students served by your school.

Positive Growth Affirmations

I Am Empowered.

I Am Energized.

I Am Enough.

I Live On Purpose.

I Make Valuable Contributions.

I Am Supported.

I Am Emotionally-Centered.

I Have The Tools I Need To Succeed.

I Learn And Improve Everyday.

I Love Myself.

About the Authors

MAATI WAFFORD is a master's level social worker who has worked in service of others on both an international and local level. She is also a Montessori educator with over 15 years serving as an educator, Independent School Leader, and Equity and Inclusion practitioner. Maati is well known for her insightful and dynamic professional development workshops and trainings she conducts, covering a variety of topics. She provides culturally-relevant support for public school start-ups, resource development, professional development and advocacy for schools in both private and public sectors across the country. She is the founder of a dynamic homeschool collective in Nashville, TN and prides herself on assisting mothers during pregnancy, labor, birth and postpartum. She has gone above and beyond the standard methods of training and professional development by dedicating herself to learn and grow as much as possible. Maati facilitates courageous conversations about ways to identify, understand, and eradicate bias amongst faculty, parents, students, and school administrators to increase critical consciousness and equity in Pre K-12 classrooms.

About the Authors

JEFF MENZISE is a proud graduate of two of our finest HBCUs, receiving his Bachelor's and Master's degrees from Fisk University in Psychology and Clinical Psychology, respectively. He finished up his academic training at Howard University majoring in Clinical Psychology with a minor in Developmental Psychology. He has worked with Ministries of Education in both the Caribbean and West Africa, providing professional development for teachers, administrators, families, students, and mental health staff. He is known locally for his dynamic presentation style, bringing insight to thousands via his community workshops, courses, and lectures. He has most recently been invited to work directly with Taraji P. Henson and her mental health foundation: The Boris Lawrence Henson Foundation. He has been featured on popular radio and television shows and in national newspapers and magazines; he is also the creator of the hit radio show "Mind on the Matter." Dr. Menzise is currently an Associate Professor with the Morgan State University Institute for Urban Research and the immediate past president of The Association of Black Psychologists, Washington, DC Chapter.

www.ingramcontent.com/pod-product-compliance
Lightning Source LLC
Chambersburg PA
CBHW061116170426
43198CB00026B/2998